ALL MY OWN STUFF

poems by
Adrian Mitchell

illustrations by
Frances Lloyd

SIMON & SCHUSTER

LONDON · SYDNEY · NEW YORK · TOKYO · SINGAPORE · TORONTO

WHAT'S THAT DOWN THERE?

What's that down there?
What's that moving?
What's that moving down in the dark
  of this chilly black maze of a cave?

Is it Sarallo —
The scarlet snake with the seven
Silver heads
And fangs that snap like a murder trap?

What's that down there?
What's that moving?
What's that moving down in the dark
  of this chilly black maze of a cave?

Is it Farranaway —
That back-cracking brute
With a hundred horns
And hoofs that hit like horrible hammers?

What's that down there?
What's that moving?
What's that moving down in the dark
  of this chilly black maze of a cave?

Is it Thilissa —
That slippery wisp of
A whispering ghost of a
Girl who died
In the moistness of mist
Which lies like a shroud on
The underground lake
down in the dark in this chilly black maze of a cave?

SONG IN SPACE

When man first flew beyond the sky
He looked back into the world's blue eye.
Man said: What makes your eye so blue?
Earth said: The tears in the ocean do.
Why are the seas so full of tears?
Because I've wept so many thousand years.
Why do you weep as you dance through space?
Because I am the Mother of the Human Race.

Rat It Up

C'mon everybody
Slap some grease on those paws
Get some yellow on your teeth
And, uh, sharpen up your claws

There's a whole lot of sausage
We're gonna swallow down
We're going to jump out the sewers
And rock this town

    Cos we're ratting it up
    Yes we're ratting it up
    Well we're ratting it up
    For a ratting good time tonight

Ain't got no compass
You don't need no map
Just follow your snout
Hey, watch out for that trap!

You can take out a poodle
You can beat up a cat
But if you can't lick a ferret
You ain't no kind of rat

    Cos we're ratting it up
    Yes we're ratting it up
    Well we're ratting it up
    For a ratting good time tonight

Now you can sneak in the henhouse
You can roll out the eggs
But if the farmer comes running
Bite his hairy legs

Check that cheese for poison
Before you eat
Or you'll wind up being served up
As ratburger meat.

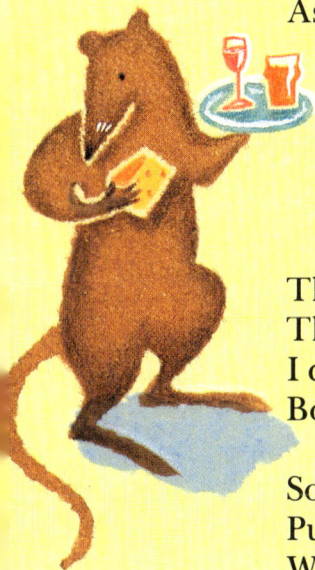

Cos we're ratting it up
Yes we're ratting it up
Well we're ratting it up
For a ratting good time tonight

This rat was born to rock
This rat was born to roll
I don't give a monkey's
Bout your pest control

So push off pussy-cat
Push off pup
We're the Rocking Rodents
And we're ratting it up

Yeah we're ratting it up
Yeah we're ratting it up
Well we're ratting it up
For a ratting good time tonight!

NOTHINGMAS DAY

No it wasn't.

It was Nothingmas Day and all the children in Notown were not tingling with excitement as they lay unawake in their heaps.
D
o
w
n
s
t
a
r
s their parents were busily not placing the last crackermugs, glimmerslips and sweetlumps on the Nothingmas Tree.

Hey! But what was that invisible trail of chummy sparks or vaulting stars across the sky?
    Father Nothingmas – drawn by 18 or 21 rainmaidens!
    Father Nothingmas – his sackbut bulging with air!
    Father Nothingmas – was not on his way!
(From the streets of the snowless town came the quiet of unsung carols and the merry silence of the steeple bell).

Next morning the children did not fountain out of bed with cries of WHOOPERATION! They picked up their Nothingmas Stockings and with traditional quiperamas such as: "Look what I haven't got! It's just what I didn't want!" pulled their stockings on their ordinary legs.

For breakfast they ate – breakfast.

8

After woods they all avoided the Nothingmas Tree,
where Daddy, his face failing to beam like a leaky torch,
was not distributing gemgames, sodaguns, golly-trolleys,
jars of humdrums and packets of slubberated croakers.

Off, off, off went the children to school, soaking each other
with no howls of "Merry Nothingmas and a Happy No
Year!", and not pulping each other with no-balls.

At school Miss Whatnot taught them how to write No
Thank You Letters.

Home they burrowed for Nothingmas Dinner.
The table was not groaning under all manner of

    NO TURKEY
    NO SPICED HAM
    NO SPROUTS
    NO CRANBERRY JELLYSAUCE
    NO NOT NOWT

There was not one (1) shoot of glee as the Nothingmas
Pudding, unlit, was not brought in. Mince pies were not
available, nor was there any demand for them.

Then, as another Nothingmas clobbered to a close, they all
haggled off to bed where they slept happily never after.

    and that is not the end of the story . . .

STUFFERATION

Lovers lie around in it
Broken glass is found in it
Grass
I like that stuff

Tuna fish get trapped in it
Legs come wrapped in it
Nylon
I like that stuff

Eskimos and tramps chew it
Madame Tussaud gave status to it
Wax
I like that stuff

Elephants get sprayed with it
Scotch is made with it
Water
I like that stuff

Clergy are dumbfounded by it
Bones are surrounded by it
Flesh
I like that stuff

Harps are strung with it
Mattresses are sprung with it
Wire
I like that stuff

Carpenters make cots of it
Undertakers use lots of it
Wood
I like that stuff

Cigarettes are lit by it
Pensioners get happy when they sit by it
Fire
I like that stuff

Dankworth's alto is made of it, most of it,
Scoobdidoo is composed of it
Plastic
I like that stuff

Apemen take it to make them hairier
I ate a ton of it in Bulgaria
Yoghurt
I like that stuff

Man-made fibres and raw materials
Old rolled gold and breakfast cereals
Platinum linoleum
I like that stuff

Skin on my hands
Hair on my head
Toenails on my feet
And linen on the bed

Well I like that stuff
Yes I like that stuff
The earth
Is made of earth
And I like that stuff

A Cat Called Slumber

In the middle of the night appears
My day-shy tabby with collapsible ears
And I stroke her head so those ears collapse
And she purrs to say that she loves me, perhaps . . .

Mrs. Christmas

She was about as small as a cup
But big as your head when she grew up
And she came to stay on Christmas Day
So we called her Mrs. Christmas

She liked to swoop around the hall
With a silver paper soccer ball
And I think I was four but maybe some more
When I named her Mrs. Christmas

She had some kittens with bright white socks
And she kept them in a brown cardboard box
And she'd nudge them out and march them about
Saying: "I am Mrs. Christmas".

11

THE WOMAN OF WATER

There once was a woman of water
Refused a Wizard her hand.
So he took the tears of a statue
And the weight from a grain of sand
And he squeezed the sap from a comet
And the height from a cypress tree
And he drained the dark from midnight
And he charmed the brains from a bee
And he soured the mixture with thunder
And stirred it with ice from hell
And the woman of water drank it down
And she changed into a well.

There once was a woman of water
Who was changed into a well
And the well smiled up at the Wizard
And down down down that old Wizard fell . . .

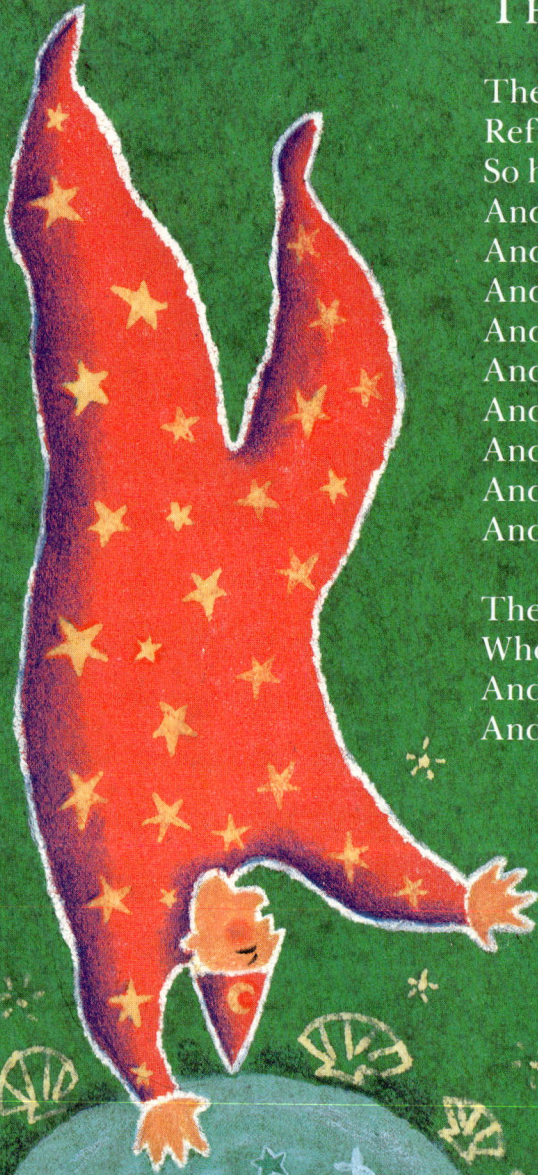

A Child is Singing

A child is singing
And nobody listening
But the child who is singing:

Bulldozers grab the earth and shower it.
  The house is on fire.
Gardeners wet the earth and flower it.
  The house is on fire.
  The houses are on fire.
Fetch the fire engine, the fire engine's on fire.
  We will have to hide in a hole.
  We will burn slow, like coal.
All the people are on fire.

And a child is singing
And nobody listening
But the child who is singing.

MY YELLOW JUMPER

When I ride a banana
At the local gymkhana
I usually win
By a skin

FRUIT JOKES

The satsuma
Has no sense of humour
But a fig'll
Giggle

SCHOOL DINNERS

Lumpy custard and liver – ugh!
I hate school dinners and I'll tell you why.
There's dog food with peas in, there's Secret Stew,
And a cheese and bacon thing we call Sick Pie.

Two-Minute Girl

(In some schools, two minutes before classes start, a Two-Minute Girl or Boy pokes his or her head round the Staffroom door and warns the teachers to Get Ready)

I'm the Two-Minute Girl
I'm about the size of a briefcase
I have bunches done up with barbed wire
And Count Dracula pointy teeth.

I'm the Two-Minute Girl
I'm as sweet as syrup pudding on the surface
But I'm as wicked as stinging nettles underneath

Two minutes early or two minutes late
I stick my head round the Staffroom door
And sometimes I whisper like the ghost of a snake
(two minutes) and leave the teachers to snore

Yes I'm the Two-Minute Girl
I'm as cunning as cunning can be
With the driving brain of a diesel train
And the mischieviousness of a flea

Oh I'm the Two-Minute Girl
I love to spread the Two-Minute Blues
Especially when I bellow TWO MINUTES!
And a teacher pours the teapot all over his new suede shoes.

I am Boj

(To be shouted, in the voice of a terrible giant,
at children who wake early)

I am Boj
I crackle like the Wig of a Judge

I am Boj
My eyes boil over with Hodge-Podge

I am Boj
Organized Sludge and a Thunder-Wedge

I am Boj
I am a Tower of solid Grudge

I am Boj
The molten Centre, the cutting Edge

I am Boj
from blackest Dudgeon I swing my Bludgeon

I am Boj

NOT A VERY CHEERFUL SONG, I'M AFRAID

There was a gloomy lady,
With a gloomy duck and a gloomy drake,
And they all three wandered gloomily,
Beside a gloomy lake,
On a gloomy, gloomy, gloomy, gloomy, gloomy, gloomy day.

Now underneath that gloomy lake
The gloomy lady's gone.
But the gloomy duck and the gloomy drake
Swim on and on and on,
On a gloomy, gloomy, gloomy, gloomy, gloomy, gloomy day.

17

GIVING POTATOES

STRONG MAN: Mashed potatoes cannot hurt you, darling
Mashed potatoes mean no harm
I have brought you mashed potatoes
From my mashed potato farm.

LADY: Take away your mashed potatoes
Leave them in the desert to dry
Take away your mashed potatoes –
You look like shepherd's pie.

BRASH MAN: A packet of chips, a packet of chips,
Wrapped in the *Daily Mail*,
Golden and juicy and fried for a week
In the blubber of the Great White Whale.

LADY: Take away your fried potatoes
Use them to clean your ears
You can eat your fried potatoes
With Birds-Eye frozen tears.

OLD MAN: I have borne this baked potato
O'er the Generation Gap,
Pray accept this baked potato
Let me lay it in your heated lap.

LADY: Take away your baked potato
In your fusty musty van
Take away your baked potato
You potato-skinned old man.

18

FRENCHMAN: She rejected all potatoes
For a thousand nights and days
Till a Frenchman wooed and won her
With pommes de terre Lyonnaises.

LADY: Oh my corrugated lover
So creamy and so brown
Let us fly across to Lyons
And lay our tubers down.

LYONS

19

THE GALACTIC PACHYDERM

The elephant stands
    among the stars
He jumps off
    Neptune
bounces off
    Mars
to adventures on
    Venus
while his children
    play
in the diamond jungles
    of the
Milky Way

AN INFANT ELEPHANT SPEAKS

I got a rusk
Stuck on my tusk

REVENGE

The elephant knocked the ground with a stick,
He knocked it slow, he knocked it quick.
He knocked it till his trunk turned black —
Then the ground turned round and knocked him back.

GIVE US A BRAKE

The runaway train knocked the buffers flat:
"Hey!" said the Stationmaster. "That's enough of that.
I've been forty-two years at this station
And I've never seen such bufferation."

THE GONDOLIERS OF GREENLAND

The Gondoliers of Greenland
Are the Grumpiest folk in the North.
Their canals melt on August the Second
And freeze up on August the Fourth.
In those two laborious glorious days
All their incomes must be made
And the rest of the year they wait listlessly
To ply their ridiculous trade.

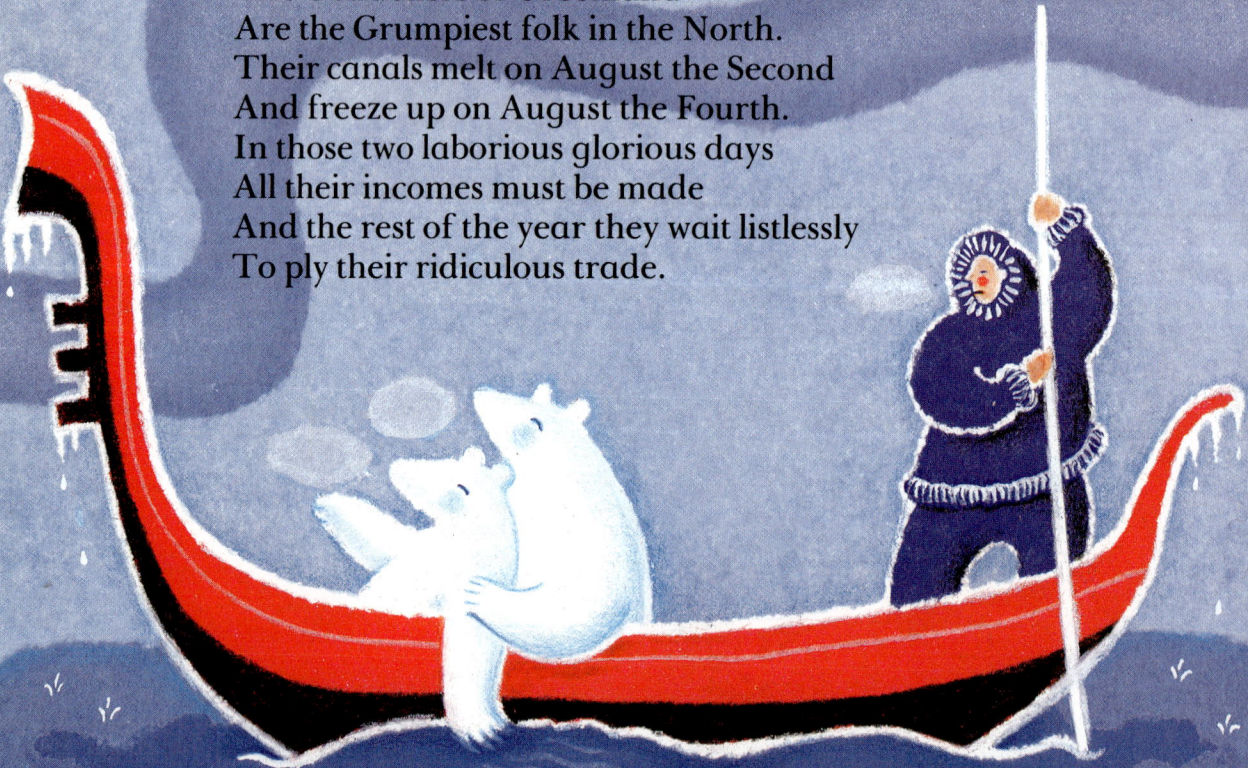

UNLUCKY STEPS

Thirteen steps
Leading me down
Down to that big blue door
Big blue door
With a grime-lined face
And a voice like a Polar bear's roar,
The sound of a mechanized blizzard
Which froze my trainers to the floor.

It sounded like a cloud of poison gas
Whispering evil to itself.
It sounded like a bunch of defrosting cobras
Slithering off their shelf.

I pushed down the handle
The handle stayed down
For three point five seconds at least
Then the handle sprang back
And the wild white sound
Of a beast that longed to be released
Suddenly stopped.

The silence swelled and swelled and swelled
As if it were about to burst.
My heart felt like a blue iced lolly
On an ice rink
In Alaska
On December the 21st.

I backed up the steps
13, 12, 11
Away from that cupboard of snows
I backed up the steps
10, 9, 8, 7
I don't want to join the Eskimos
I backed up the steps
6, 5, 4
My blood saying: Go man, go man!
I backed up the steps
Then I turned around –
That's when I got eaten by a snowman.

A Speck Speaks

About ten million years ago
I was a speck of rock in a vast black rock.
My address was:
    Vast Black Rock,
    Near Italy,
    Twelve Metres Under
The Mediterranean Sea.

The other specks and I
Formed an impressive edifice –
Bulbously curving at the base
With rounded caves
And fun tunnels for the fish,
Romantically jagged at the top.

Life, for us specks, was uneventful –
One for all, welded together
In the cool, salty wet.
What more could specks
Expect?

One day, it was a Wednesday I remember
A scampi flicked me off my perch
Near the vast black rock's peak
And I was scurried down
Long corridors of currents
Until a wave caught me in its mouth
And spat me out on –
What?

A drying stretch
Of yellow, white, black, red and transparent specks,
Billions of particles,
Loosely organized in bumps and dips;
Quite unlike the tight hard group
Which I belonged to in the good old rock.
Heat banged down on us all day long.
Us? I turned to the speck next to me,
A lumpish red fellow who'd been washed off a brick.

"I'm new here," I confessed,
"What are we supposed to be?"
He bellowed back –
(But the bellow of a speck
Is less than the whispering of ants) –
"We're grains now, grains of sand,
And this society is called Beach."

"Beach?" I said. "What are we grains supposed to do?"
"Just stray around, lie loose,
Go with the wind, go with the sea
And sink down when you're trodden on."

"Don't know if I can manage that.
Used to belong to Vast Black Rock
And we all stuck together."

"Give Beach a try," said the red grain.
Well, there was no alternative.

Many eras later
I was just beginning to feel
Part of Beach, that slow-drifting,
Slow-shifting, casual community,
When I was shovelled up
With a ton of fellow grains,
Hoisted into a lorry, shaken down a road,
Washed, sifted and poured in a machine
Hotter than the sunshine.

When they poured me out, life had changed again.
My mates and I swam in a molten river
Down into a mould.
White-hot we were, then red, then
Suddenly cold
And we found ourselves merged
Into a tall, circular tower,
Wide at the bottom, narrow at the top
What's more, we'd all turned green as sea-weed.
Transparent green.
We had become – a wine bottle.

In a few flashes of time
We'd been filled with wine,
Stoppered, labelled, bumped to a shop,
Stood in a window, sold, refrigerated,
Drained by English tourists,
Transmogrified into a lampstand,
Smashed by a four-year-old called Tarquin,
Swept up, chucked in the garbage, hauled away,
Dumped and bulldozed into the sea.

Now the underwater years sandpaper away
My shield-shaped fragment of bottle.
So one day I shall be a single grain again,
A single grain of green, transparent glass.

When that day comes
I will transmit a sub-aquatic call
To all green specks of glass
Proposing that we form
A Vast Green Rock of Glass,
Near Italy,
Twelve Metres Under
The Mediterranean Sea.

Should be pretty spectacular
In about ten million years.

All being well.

FOR NUMBER TEN

One out of ten, six gold, four black.
Born in a bulging, transparent sack.

I eased him out, this holy gift.
His mother turned to him and sniffed

Then licked the blood and the sack away.
All small and golden, there he lay.

There are some insects and some flowers
Whose life is spent in twenty-four hours.

For twenty-four hours, beside his mother,
He fed and he slept with his sisters and brothers.

Good smells. Close warm. Then a crushing weight.
Then nothing at all. His head the wrong shape.

He was wrapped up and taken beyond the bounds
Of his mother's familiar digging grounds

For she would have found him and known him too
And have wept as golden retrievers do.

So she kept all her love for the alive –
The black four and the golden five.

But I celebrate that golden pup
Whom I talked to and kissed as I wrapped him up.

For he fed and he slept and was loved as he lay
In the dark where he spent one golden day.

Now his mother pursues an eccentric trail
With casual sweeps of her lavish gold tail

And when number ten stumbles into my mind
She consoles me and so do the other nine.

TO MY DOG

This gentle beast
This golden beast
laid her long chin
along my wrist

and my wrist
is branded
with her love
and trust

and the salt of my cheek
is hers to lick
so long as I
or she shall last

POEMS IN THIS BOOK

ACKNOWLEDGEMENTS
Some poems in this book have previously appeared in *Nothingmas Day*
(Allison & Busby), *Out Loud* (Writers and Readers Cooperative), *Poems*,
Ride the Nightmare and *The Apeman Cometh* (Jonathan Cape) and
Strawberry Drums (Simon & Schuster Young Books).

Adrian Mitchell is a writer of poems, stories and plays for both adults and children. He started writing when he was nine and nobody has been able to stop him.

Frances Lloyd, a talented newcomer to children's book illustration, was born in Tallaght, Eire. She holds a BA Hons. degree in Graphic Design from Newcastle-upon-Tyne Polytechnic and has undertaken commissions for advertising and magazine illustration.

Also published
Strawberry Drums
A book of poems put together by Adrian Mitchell
Illustrated by Frances Lloyd
Hardback ISBN 0-7500-0356-1 Paperback ISBN 0-7500-0364-2